through time
Sydney

JEFFREY St

Rolf Heimann

Roland Harvey Books
92 Bay Street
Port Melbourne
Victoria 3207
Australia

Roland Harvey Books is an imprint of Roland Harvey Studios

First Published 1999

Designed by Roland Harvey Studios

Film by Eray Scan, Singapore.
Printed in Hong Kong and produced by Phoenix Offset.

National Library of Australia Cataloguing-in-Publication data:

Heimann, Rolf, 1940-
    Sydney through time.
    ISBN 0 949714 67 4.
    1. Puzzles – Juvenile literature. 2. Sydney (N.S.W.) –
    History – Juvenile literature. I. Title.
    994.41

Welcome to Sydney
Follow its history, solve its mystery...

A city can be looked at as a piece of art, not created by one person alone, or even by a single generation, but by all the people who ever lived there. Town planners may see themselves as makers of a city, but it is the people who are truly its creators. Sydney is a perfect illustration of this.

When, under instructions from Captain Arthur Phillip, the German surveyor Augustus Theodore Von Alt laid out the first street plans, he imagined an orderly planned city quite unlike the one that soon sprouted up. Short cuts between major points established new lanes, and inconvenient streets were unused. A living city responds to the ever-changing needs of a community. It will adopt unforeseen inventions, open itself up to new discoveries and welcome diverse newcomers.

I first saw the city of Sydney in 1959 and I thought it was one of the most beautiful places I had ever seen. The Sydney Harbour Bridge was one of the first things I ever sketched in Australia.

I have come back to Sydney dozens of times since then, by train, by bus, by plane and in big ships, and several times even navigating through the heads myself. Each time the city has changed. And even unwelcome changes cannot destroy Sydney's magic.

This book is gratefully dedicated to all those who helped create this wonderful work of art called Sydney, from the long-suffering convicts who 200 years ago laboured to lay its foundations, to the latest arrivals who bring their own varied backgrounds and experiences to the city. And to the Aboriginal people who for thousands of years have lived within and around its boundaries.

I want to pay a special tribute to some of the people who have had a hand in creating Sydney. And being a creator of puzzle books, I want to do it in my own personal way by hiding their names in the pictures. For example, look for the lizard in each double page spread and follow the letters next to it, on each page, until the end of the book. This will spell the name 'Arthur Phillip'. Do the same for the butterfly, the mouse, the bird, the heart, the eight-pointed star and the peace symbol and you will have the names of other Sydney figures. If you're uncertain, glance at page 32.

And, of course, I've hidden the map of Australia on each double page, as I've done ever since I became an Australian citizen. You might even find me hidden in the pictures!

Thousands of years ago

During the last Ice Age, which began about 40 000 years ago, the sea level was about a hundred metres lower than it is today, and what is now Sydney Harbour was just a valley crossed by streams.

Many millions of years before the first people came to Australia there were wallabies eight times the size of those today, and the wombat-like diprotodon was larger than a rhinoceros. This animal still existed when the first people came to Australia over 40 000 years ago. During the last Ice Age the Aboriginal people actually walked on the bottom of Sydney Harbour!

Before 1788

About 6000 years ago the area took on its present shape. The people who lived here called themselves the Eoa. They were divided into several tribes which met to trade and to hold religious ceremonies. These ceremonies were called corroborees and they were held at night by the light of campfires.

1788

Like all the Aboriginal people of Australia, the Eoa were skilled trackers, hunters and fishermen.

They did not build permanent settlements, but roamed their area according to the seasons. Their shelters were usually made of bark and they also used large sheets of it to construct their canoes. They lived undisturbed for many thousands of years until February 1788, when Captain Arthur Phillip came to explore the harbour in two small boats.

9

1789

Captain Arthur Phillip set up camp near a freshwater
stream in a little bay which he called Sydney Cove.

He had been sent by the King of England to establish an English penal colony.

So that he could talk with the native people, Captain Phillip ordered some of them to be captured and taught English. One of those Aboriginal men was called Bennelong, and he later accompanied Captain Phillip to England, where he was introduced to the King.

1814

The first house on the North Shore, opposite Sydney Cove, was built by free settler James Milson. At first James was disappointed that his fifty acres were mostly stony ground, but then he turned the rocks into profit by selling them as ballast to departing sailing ships.

In May 1814 the ship, *Three Bees*, with fourteen loaded guns aboard it, caught fire. As the mooring line burned through, the ship began to drift across the harbour while its cannons went off.

One of these shots hit Milson's new boat shed!

1836

The famous convict architect Francis Greenway had designed magnificent stables for the governor. They were so spectacular that the governor's horses seemed to be housed more splendidly than the governor himself! This sore point was remedied in 1836 when the Colonial Office in England sent over the plans for a new government house. It was not built until 1842.

By 1836 Australians had developed a love for swimming. The Colonial Government found this practice indecent and it imposed heavy fines on anyone who was found in the water between the hours of six in the morning and six in the evening.

But that did not stop Australians from enjoying the water!

1879

The International Exhibition of 1879 was a major event for Sydney. It was housed in the 'Garden Palace' and one of its towers contained Australia's first hydraulic lift. Steam-powered trams replaced horse-drawn ones to bring travellers from the railway station. People came from as far away as Melbourne, which had been connected by rail since 1874.

The event was spoiled by rain. Three years later rain would have been welcome – the Garden Palace burned to the ground. The heat was so intense that it cracked window panes in Macquarie Street.

1904

This was the year when the Electric Power Station at Pyrmont was completed and electricity became generally available. Sydney's first trams had been horse-drawn, then steam-powered, now they became electric. A tram depot replaced the old Fort Macquarie on Bennelong Point. When electricians installed cables underneath Sydney's Town Hall they discovered a coffin with a body inside it! The building had been erected on the site of the old cemetery and at the time it was assumed that all coffins had been removed. But now the workers put a bottle with the day's newspaper on the corpse and poured cement over the coffin. It is still there!

Sydney's first aerial photograph from a balloon was taken in 1904.

1931

By 1931 hundreds of houses had been demolished during construction of the Sydney Harbour Bridge. Ferry operators opposed the bridge, believing it would bring ferry transport to an end. This was not so, as ferries remain the best way to reach certain areas of the harbour.

Sixteen people suffered fatal accidents during construction. One worker who fell from a great height into the water survived, because, so he believed, he made swimming motions through the air! When the bridge was opened in March 1932, a military officer dashed forward on his horse and cut the ribbon before the state's premier could do so.

The officer was arrested and charged with 'destroying a ribbon worth two pounds' and was fined five pounds plus court costs.

1942

In 1942 the post office tower suddenly disappeared. The government feared that as it was the highest building of the time, it could give Sydney's position away to the enemy during World War II. All the stones were numbered before being put into storage.

To help the war effort, many restrictions were imposed. Waistcoats and double-breasted suits were banned, as were patterns on socks, and belts wider than two inches. It was illegal for advertisers to mention Christmas, and Christmas cakes were allowed only if they did not look like Christmas cakes. Even pink icing on wedding cakes was forbidden! Sydney signposts were removed, so as to confuse the Japanese should they try to invade. Foreigners were once more imprisoned.

In May 1942 three small Japanese submarines entered Sydney Harbour. Before they were destroyed, they managed to sink a ship, killing nineteen people.

VICTORY

1964

It was not until 1964 that the post office tower graced Sydney's skyline once more. Prime Minister Menzies joked that it was a rare occasion indeed when one could put the clock back!

Sydney was to receive another landmark with its famous Opera House. A total of 223 entries from 30 countries had been considered before Joern Utzon's design was chosen.

The first performance was held before the building was even finished, when the American singer Paul Robeson sang on the construction site for the workers.

1988

This was the year when Sydney and Australia celebrated its two hundredth birthday. The gathering of tall ships was just one of many events of the year.

But there were also demonstrations by Australian Aborigines fighting for recognition that they owned the land long before Europeans arrived.

2000

Many Sydneysiders were proud
when their city was chosen to
host the Olympic Games.

Some Sydney landmarks, past and present, which are featured in this book.

First Government House

Built in 1788, with several extensions in later years. For instance, a veranda was added in 1802. Demolished in 1845 after construction of the new Government House in the Domain.

Dawes Gun Battery

This fortification was started by Lieutenant William Dawes in 1788 as the first shore defence of Sydney. It was modified several times and it finally made way for the south pylons of the Harbour Bridge. Remnants of the fort and old cannons can still be inspected.

Tank Stream Bridge

Australia's first stone bridge, it replaced an earlier wooden one which collapsed under an overloaded cart. Finished in 1804. Builders were paid in 675 gallons of rum instead of money!

First Saint Phillips Church

Foundation stone laid in 1800. In 1806 the tower was destroyed by fire and it had to be rebuilt. The church opened on Christmas Day 1810.

St James Church

Designed by Francis Greenway as the Court House, then changed into a church. Opened in 1824.

Fort Macquarie

Built in 1817 from locally quarried stone, it had 15 heavy guns, and was in working order until 1900. Bennelong's hut was here, and the site is named after him. Now the site of the Sydney Opera House.

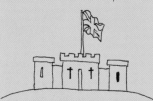

Commissariat Store

Building began in 1809, finished in 1812. Demolished in 1940. It was for many years one of the most important buildings on Circular Quay and housed government supplies.

Governor's Stables

Designed by convict architect Francis Greenway. Started in 1816 and finished in 1821. In 1915 the central courtyard was roofed as a concert hall for the Sydney Music Conservatory. It is still undergoing periodic alterations.

Second Government House

Designed in England by Queen Victoria's favourite architect, Edward Blore. Started in 1836, the first stage was finished in 1842. It underwent many extensions and alterations. It was the home of the state's governors until 1996.

Second St Phillips Church

Designed by Edmund Blacket. Begun in 1848, finished in 1856. Work had to be interrupted in 1851 when all stonemasons left for the goldfields!

Sydney Observatory

Built in 1858 on Observatory Hill. The site had earlier been used for a windmill and as a fort and signal station. Since 1858 a black ball has been dropped from its tower to mark 1pm. It used to be followed by a gunshot from Fort Denison, and Sydneysiders set their watches by it.

Town Hall

First foundation stone 1868. Finished in 1889. Built on the site of a cemetery. When electric wiring was added in 1904, another coffin was found. A bottle with a newspaper of the day was put into this coffin, then cemented over. It is still there!

Mort's Wool House

For many years a major landmark on Circular Quay. It made way for the AMP building which was finished in 1962.

Customs House

Built in 1888 on the site of the earlier customs house. The clock was added in 1897. Since 1997 a cultural centre.

Lands Department Building

Designed by James Barnet, who created many of Sydney's most admired buildings. Built in 1877, the tower was added later. The exterior has 48 niches for explorers and politicians responsible for promoting settlement, 25 of them are still vacant!

Garden Palace

Constructed in 1879 for the International Exhibition, burned down in 1882. One tower contained Sydney's first hydraulic lift. A steam-powered tram replaced the horse-drawn one to bring passengers from the railway station.

General Post Office

One of Sydney's most magnificent buildings. Its 'keystone' weighed over 26 tons. The first stage was completed in 1874. Extensions, including the 73 m high tower, were completed in 1890. For many years it was Sydney's tallest building. The tower was dismantled in 1942 and re-erected in 1964.

A.S.N. Co. Building

Designed by the Melbourne architect William Wardell. Built in 1884, it is still one of the main landmarks of the Rocks.

Queen Victoria Building

Built in 1898 as a produce market. It had several other uses, including city library. Demolition was considered, but the building was saved as an arcade for 200 shops. Pierre Cardin called it the most beautiful shopping centre in the world!

Fort Macquarie Tram Terminal

Built in 1902 replacing Fort Macquarie. Pulled down in 1958 to make way for the Opera House.

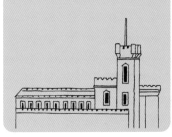

Australian Temperance and General Mutual Life Insurance Company Building

Built in 1932, demolished around 1975. For a time it was not only Sydney's tallest building but the one with the longest name!

Sydney Harbour Bridge

The proposal for this bridge was accepted in 1922 and it was finished in 1932. Three steam ships were built to transport 42 000 tons of granite. 1400 workers were employed, 16 of them were accidentally killed. 15 000 tons of steel were used. Each coat of paint needs 30 000 litres!

AWA Building

The steel radio mast on top made it Sydney's highest building from 1938 until the 1960s. Flashing lights signalled the weather forecast.

Maritime Services Building

Built 1947-52. In 1988 it became the Museum of Contemporary Art.

AMP Building

Built in 1962, it was then Sydney's tallest building (26 storeys). A second, taller AMP building was built some years later.

Opera House

223 designs from 30 countries were received. The Danish architect Joern Utzon was announced as the winner of the design competition in 1957. Opened in 1973 in the presence of Queen Elizabeth II.

MLC Centre

Designed by Harry Seidler, completed in 1978. It has 65 columnless floors.

AMP Tower

Part of the Centrepoint shopping centre, completed in 1981. For many years Australia's highest structure at 305 metres, it is supported by 56 cables, each weighing 7 tons. Racing up the 1474 stairs has become a yearly Sydney sporting event.

Some of Sydney's creators

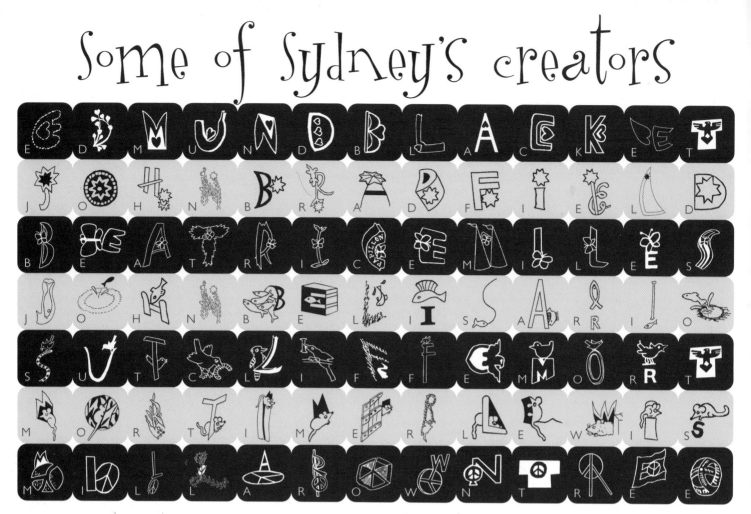

EDMUND BLACKET

JOHN BRADFIELD

BEATRICE MILES

JOHN BELISARIO

SUTCLIFFE MORT

MORTIMER LEWIS

MILLA ROWNTREE

Edmund Blacket became Colonial Architect in 1849. Apart from creating Sydney University and working on other important projects, he designed 58 churches, (including the second St Phillips, begun in 1848). For this reason he has sometimes been called 'the Christopher Wren of Australia'.

John Bradfield designed the Sydney Harbour Bridge and supervised its construction. Proposals for a bridge were first submitted to him in 1911 when he was Chief Engineer of the Metropolitan Railway Construction. His design was approved in 1922. The bridge was finished in 1932.

Beatrice Miles commonly known as Bea Miles, was an eccentric Sydney character, who died in 1972, aged 71. Coming from a well-to-do family, Bea was a brilliant university student, but at the age of 21 she was committed to a mental asylum and stayed there for 3 years. She then chose a life on the streets and was constantly in trouble with the police for minor offences like riding a bicycle in an evening dress while blowing a policeman's whistle. She conducted her own defence with great eloquence. Right up to an old age she frequented libraries and remained well-read, being able to quote Shakespeare at length.

John Belisario has been called the Father of Australian Dentistry. In 1847 he pioneered the use of ether, 8 months after its discovery in America. It has been said that the monuments to him are the teeth of Sydneysiders!

Sutcliffe Mort arrived in Sydney in 1838, aged 22. He exported wool and meat and was ridiculed for his experiments with creating 'artificial frost'. He died in 1878 before his belief was vindicated. English newspapers reported in 1880 that the first shipment of frozen meat from Australia arrived in excellent condition.

Mortimer Lewis was Colonial Architect and he supervised the construction of the second Government House. He modified the design of the building which had been planned in England by Edward Blore.

Milla Rowntree is not famous, but she is one of the many Sydneysiders who have been good to me over the years. Milla saved my life by taking me (against my will) to hospital when she correctly diagnosed a fractured skull after a riding accident! The other reason for her inclusion here is that she has thirteen letters to her name.